G000055160

SHADOW CAST BY MOUNTAINS

24 2 05

Shadow Cast by Mountains

Patrick Howse

Hayloft Publishing Ltd
Kendal, Cumbria

First published 2017 Hayloft Publishing Ltd.

A CIP catalogue record for this book is available from the British Library

ISBN 978–1–910237–33–5

Printed and bound by Bell and Bain Ltd, Glasgow
Frontispiece image by Inge Schlaile

Hayloft policy is to use papers that are natural, renewable and recyclable products and made from wood grown in sustainable forests. The logging and manufacturing processes are expected to conform to the environmental regulations of the country of origin.

Hayloft Publishing Ltd,
a company registered in England number 4802586
2 Staveley Mill Yard, Staveley, Kendal, LA8 9LR (registered office)
L'Ancien Presbytère, 21460 Corsaint, France (editorial office)

Email: books@hayloft.eu
+44 (0) 7971 352473 (UK)
+33 (0) 380 89 760 (Fr)

www.hayloft.eu

To Inge
Who found me broken
And rescued me
With love

Contents

Foreword

The last time I worked with Patrick Howse, we were standing in a street outside the heavily overstocked and stinking city mortuary in Baghdad, and my mouth was so dry with fear that I was having trouble getting my words out as I talked to camera.

Patrick was the producer.

Given that it was likely that someone would turn up and kill us at any moment, he was very restrained. It must have been agonising.

This kind of work in places like Baghdad takes its toll. Patrick has found an elegant way of coping with the pressures and strains: he has turned it into poetry and prose.

I've found writing a pretty effective therapy myself, but it doesn't always work. I can't rid myself of the memory of an Iraqi man who described to me how he sold almost everything he had in the world to pay a ransom for his kidnapped brother; when he went to pick him up and bring him home, he found only his body, mutilated for some sadist's enjoyment.

Writing hasn't much helped me with that one; sometimes when I wake up in the night it's my brother who's lying there, tortured to death – only I don't have a brother.

Patrick must get a lot of people telling him how glamorous his life is. It's not. It's highly pressurised, it can often be terrifying, and it takes a big toll on your personal life. And even when you're far away from a place like Baghdad, Baghdad comes to you.

John Simpson

Introduction

I was born into a world still reeling from the effects of war. Both my grandfather and father had at one time earned a living killing Germans.

For a child growing up in the 1960s and 70s 'THE war' was everywhere, from watching *The Great Escape* and *The Dambusters* on TV, to "playing army" in the woods and fields near my house. It is only now, in my fifties, that I have an inkling how difficult it must have been for my father to watch me grow up.

Shadow Cast By Mountains is a collection that grew out of the Iraq war, which I covered for the BBC between 2003 and 2009. I regard the book as a single, extended narrative: it tells the story of the world I was born into; my war and how it changed me; and the world that emerged from the wreckage.

I think British poetry has not adequately addressed the conflicts of the recent past, or at least not with any degree of intellectual honesty or emotional continence. I'm trying to occupy that vacant space.

That is not to say that the poems are "about" that war – I'm not trying to be Wilfred Owen (much as I admire him). However, they are almost all coloured by that and other conflicts, and one of my inspirations is Edward Thomas.

The book comes in three parts: Long Slow Betrayals, which examines the legacy of the First and Second World Wars, and the drift towards the "War on Terror"; A New Life, which looks at my personal and psychological reaction to that war; and A Winter Comes, which is inspired by the world Vladimir Putin and Donald Trump are trying to create.

I'd like to thank my publisher, Dawn Robertson, for her help and encouragement.

I'd also like to thank my children, Eleanor, Joseph and Clara – their love and their commitment to creativity are a constant joy to me.

Patrick Howse

Munich, Easter 2017

PART I
Long Slow Betrayals

Pendle Hill, Patrick Howse

Bashall Eaves

After the war that took the fathers
But before the next
Had taken their sons,

A man was murdered here:
Shot with a hand-moulded bullet
Fired from a home-made gun.

The village knew killer and killed,
But bled the mystery bit by bit
Deep into Bowland soil.

Young, I came long after
To the old stone houses
Enclosing a triangle of green.

Breathless and rosy cheeked
A girl I'd never met
And would never see again

Handed me a single red flower;
Then, smiling, she walked away,
Knowing this village keeps its secrets.

Bowland Sunset

The sun dived
Into a western sea
Showering me with gold;

Lavender shadows
Lengthened to purple
The hollows of the hills.

The night came
Glacially, a new ice age
Filling black valleys;

My empty hand
Vainly sought
A returned clasp.

Later, much later,
Far away,
I found it.

Belfast

Midsummer evenings
Are long and golden;
The sun sets behind

Sensuously rounded hills,
Burnishing the heather
And the army post.

The sky settles for
Shades either side
Of dying yellow,

But spreads a
Stain of night
Through resentful streets.

Christmas Pudding

You have to know a good recipe,
But also what can be added
And what can be left out;

You have to buy all the ingredients
And then go back
And buy the ones you've forgotten;

You have to mix thoroughly
With five hundred
Years of tradition

And unarticulated yearning
For lost childhood
And dead parents;

You have to steam it for eight hours
And forget it for two months,
Then heat it and set it alight

And watch blue flame dance
On its dome like a demon
On a cathedral roof;

Then you have to eat and eat and eat
Until all that's left is the expectation
You'll do it again next year.

Mrs MacDonald Visits Her Father

She felt the ebbing tide
And went to the loch shore
To gather sea shells.

She last saw him
Marching off, tall
To her, and special,

But smaller with every step
He took away from her,
Unremarked in kilted uniform.

Soon he was nothing more
Than just another
Claggy lump of Belgium.

From eighty hard
Highland winters she came
To a green field

He knew only as mud
To bend painful knees
To kneel before him,

And arranged her shells
To spell out one word –
DADDY.

Birka, Island of the Birches, Patrick Howse

Birka, Island of the Birches

Every shade of blue
Broken by white glare
Smashing the sea-sky-mirror
With dazzle.

Grass mounds left
By men departed,
Gone a-viking,
Bear witness

Beneath standing
Stones and two trees
Seemingly growing
From one root.

Looking closer, now,
From a distance,
I see they always
Grew apart.

Moles in the War Cemetery

The mist blanket
Tucked round the graves
Relents only slowly
To the wan autumn sun.

The rows of
Disciplined stones await
The parade regimentally,
Perfect in eternal ranks.

Two new corpses,
Blind eyes forever closed,
Lie freshly on
The Portland slab.

Pristine in black velvet,
Large hands spread
In futile supplication,
Noses pointing to heaven.

Metalwork

He tried to make a garden
Where the sun would grow:

He toiled moving earth
And digging sand and compost

Into soil he thought
The flowers might favour.

But slowly, season by season,
Life and light failed:

Only the chill and the darkness thrived,
Only the shadows bloomed;

The blackness set hard
In cooled molten lead.

Plague Village

A low winter sun
Kisses grassy mounds
And casts their feet
Into pools of purple shadow.

Alone now the church
Built by these gone people
Bears witness, surrounded
By empty fields.

A tree stands
Branches lopped
Head bowed
Crucified.

Plague Village, Patrick Howse

Washington (February 2003)

Unrelenting snow
smothers a nation's
proud landmarks.

Alone I wade through
waist-deep drifts
piled higher,

imprisoning Lincoln
and Jefferson, and
shutting down the city.

The Mansion, its lawn
white as its walls
and columns,

defined by black
separating spiked railings;
and between

the icon and my cold
wet feet, a heap stirs,
a termites' nest

hesitantly moves,
cascading small avalanches
down dishevelled slopes:

a man, newborn,
emerges from his
pavement, stands up

and shakes the cruel
two day blizzard
slowly, very slowly

from his
beaten, bowed,
sack-covered back.

Washington DC, Patrick Howse

The Outrage

It's not that
We forget,

It's how easily
We accept

Just another

Slab

He lies
flat quiet
in ice
cooled calm.

They go
off into
the world
without him.

Another England

Mistaken for gusting leaves
Swirling mice chase
Around each other
Across paths at dusk;

A fox trots insolently
From hunger-shredded sacks
Leaving rubbish strewn
Across trimmed gardens;

Seagulls view picnics
With yellow eyes,
While behind the skirtings
Rats scratch busily.

There before us,
There when we've gone,
Their waves touch ours
Out of phase:

More wildly visceral,
Savage but less cruel,
Another England rustles
In still night woods.

Aglonquin Park

Past a bear-paw-print,
up the track through trees,
pushed by a thrilling howl
to a summit.

Below, a lake made by
beavers drowning pines
and birches meanders
to grassland.

And beyond, a ridge,
wooded like this one,
bathed in the threat -
the actual promise -

of wolves and moose
and black bears.
And then northwards
line after line of

forested passes
disregarded by a
woman, and a girl,
there on the peak.

I feel the companionship
of the ravens, the eagles,
and the wild woods
fading away forever.

How He Notices Everything

All the colours in her eyes.
Murmuring distant traffic.
A sky washed blue.

The rattling Underground,
Grinding building site,
Salt-dew wetness of sweat

Breaking, dotted notes
Resounding in hollowness;
A sprung rhythm

Pounding in his ears,
Beating irregular time,
Counting down.

Now, just now,
Finally now,
He notices everything.

Statues of Generals

Journey through
The subconscious
Of men who
Commission statues:

Turn your back
On the glories
Of Trafalgar,
And walk down Whitehall.

Slim stares all
The way to Burma
Without the need
Of binoculars;

Montgomery scowls
At Downing Street
As Alanbrooke
Averts his gaze;

Haig is on a horse,
Its foot raised,
Trampling.

The Wounds of General Freyberg

The gallant youth
Paid in advance
For all the letters
After his name.

Unstintingly he mingled
His blood with
His spilled generation;
Patched up and bandaged

But never wholly healed,
He was sent off
To do it all again
In one war, then another.

Finally the old man
Settled his account:
Wounds from the Somme
Opened up like

The bared soul
Of a confessing sinner,
And from his deepest scars
Blood flowed, unstoppable.

That Summer

The paving stones
Shiver heat

And hushed streets
Lie stunned,

Aghast.

Berkeley Square

My long-dead mother's horror
Of rat-filled bomb-shelters,
Her claustrophobia, her chilblains,
Hit me in a Blitz blast-wave,

Intruding into my middle age.
When I stumble
Across the name-plate
I hear the words and refrain,

I feel the wartime sentimental
Longing for nightingales,
And wonder
If nostalgia is inherited.

The Balvenie

Smooth tawny peppery fire
whispers of a bottle
in a bottom drawer
of a desk,

opened and sipped
on hot evenings
to an accompaniment
of murder.

I sip still in the evening
watching the level lower,
watching it slowly
run out.

For Grant Henderson

Television Centre, W12

This building was the factory
Where television made the glue
That stuck our nation together.

Now silver foil peels from Space Age
Air conditioning ducts
And a blue tit flits into a broken-
Brick hole to build this spring's nest.

A suspended walkway bridges
The intersecting curves
Of Modernism and Futurism,

And spans the gap between
The optimism born before I was,
And the decrepit worn-out cynicism
Of our already tired century.

Tawny Owl

She sits in a spindly lane-side tree,
Plump and delightfully pompous,
Chest feathers aristocratically ruffled.
Her brown mottled plumage

Is as neat and cuddly as a cat,
And her doze-narrowed eyes
Shine blackly into the spring twilight;
I dare not breathe...

A rude aggressive chatter
Of a chaffinch breaks the spell.
Startled fully awake, the owl's eyes
Open to a penetrating expression

Of human righteous outrage:
A duchess with a pinched bottom,
She gathers up her dignity like a shawl
And flies silently into the coming night.

Future Tense

(A glimpse of the best you can hope for)

I'm waiting to watch doctors
Burn a vein from my leg.
I sit in blue support stockings
Fretfully killing time
Beside a well made bed, while
Spring streams through the window.

A curtain cordons my left,
But across the ward a mirror
Image bed and chair face me:
There lies a man.
Elderly, grey hair, grey complexion,
Gaping black chasm of a mouth

Pointing upwards as he snores
Softly in pressed pyjamas;
Clean shaven, brushed hair,
Thin ankles, bony feet
Stretch towards me beyond the
End-of-bed charts and clinical space.

By his side sits a neat
Woman in white cardigan,
Very quietly watching his face
As her hand holds his
And her thumb gently strokes
His skinny white-wizened knuckles.

She looks away now,
Far away to spring, to the emerging
Daisies and the fading daffodils
To singing birds and
Benign sunshine, brought in by the breeze
Creeping through the window and rustling the blinds.

The Flood, the Seagull and the Rat

The Thames flows towards its highest tide, gently
Lapping over its bank from Hammersmith to Kew.
The river is determined, for now,

Not to flow to the sea, but to follow its tidal impulse
And make a lake of its floodplain.
Still the tide rises, the majestic water flowing
Unhurried, but with enormous force

The wrong way, upstream, suddenly recognisable
As an Amazon or a Nile separating Middlesex from Surrey.
Each minute each smug shore drifts further apart.

Gulls float on the body of the water, passively allowing
It to take them wherever it wishes.
One, her breast as white and fluffy as a kitten,
Her slate grey back as harsh as

A goose-stepping Prussian, catches
Something from the glinting silver-brown surface.
In her savage yellow bill she grips a rat.

She manoeuvres the wriggling body until the snout
Begins its jerky journey down the chasm-throat.
Now feeble pawing feet are on the brink,
The tail thrashing as the rat wonders

Whether this is quite the sort of dark
Passageway he fancies slipping down to explore.
With a Serengeti-wild abruptness he's gone,

And the bright eye of the gull sparkles
As she bobs slightly lower in the water,
And preens with her razor beak
The imperfections from the self-satisfied feathers.

Appeased, the water slowly becomes still,
And imperceptibly turns back
To flow to the sea.

A Dream About Iraq

Deer are being culled,
Their bodies piled on the heather,
Dumped on one another.
A new born fawn stumbling,

Shot through the leg, limping,
Bullet holes weeping,
Dark wide eyes staring.
I wake smelling blood.

Kuwait

A pressed down
Heat exhausted stagger
Through furnace-fierce oppression.

The implacable sun
Beats down slave labour
Squatting in hot shade.

A panting sparrow
Falls limp from a
Dust heavy palm tree.

It's flaccid tongue
Hangs out impotently
From a gaping beak.

For Chris Booth

Evolution

We gave English to the world,
So she no longer belongs to us:
Mumbai and Lagos and Shanghai
Will truss her up and take her
To strange, exotic places.

The only constant is eternal change,
But where there's life
There will probably be beetles,
And the place of rats will be taken
By something quite rat-like.

Perhaps there will always be feathers,
So that long after the last kingfisher's death
His flashing glint of brilliance
Might live on further
In some new creature.

And so the language of Chaucer
Continues to evolve towards extinction,
Towards a new language incomprehensible to us:
But perhaps we might recognise
A far-distant glint of feathers.

Wayland's Smithy

The Saxons came late
To land still owned by
Generations of eloquent dead.

They recognised divinity
here, before this
was England.

The far horizon is weighted
with waves of rain,
but sunlight picks out russet

From the green-gold leaves
of giant sentinels dwarfed
by the age of stone.

The Distance Between Souls

We walk towards each other with closed faces
In isolated internal worlds
With secret, unarticulated sorrows,
Unvoiced joys and the insular

Passions of unshared lives.
At the atomic level it's impossible
To touch; the forces of the universe
Physically repel us from one another.

We can hope for fleeting connections
Through love or art or intellect,
But I'm overwhelmed by the sadness
In the distance between souls.

The Gusts – Baghdad

I knew it was coming.
The Green Zone sirens
Blared their warning
Calling out across the ancient Tigris
Spreading gentle ripples of terror
Through the womb of history.

I felt it speeding.
Through the dusty orange air
I heard it roaring
Making its cartoon clichéd wail
As it rushed to meet its noisy rendezvous
With a haphazard crash site.

Then I felt it screaming.
But still it hadn't reached me
I felt it, shivering,
Holding my breath in anticipation
Of the hot blast
That I couldn't escape.

In my face the fiery passing.
A slap-like blow
In an instant leaving
Clouds of debris and smoke
As my choking breath escaped
And everything went black.

Loch Lubnaig, Patrick Howse

The Gusts – Loch Lubnaig

I saw it coming.
First the wave it made along the surface
I saw it running
Along the water of the Loch
Scattering shining shards of light
Across the length of the water.

Then I heard it whispering.
In the waving branches
I heard it murmuring
In the pine trees that stood
Close by the side of the path
Casting their dark blue shadows.

Then I felt it coming.
But still it hadn't reached me
I felt it, shivering,
Holding my breath in anticipation
Of the cold blast
That I couldn't escape.

In my face the icy passing.
A slap-like blow
In an instant leaving,
Leaping on down the valley
As my breath escaped
And the sun shone.

Pennies

The shape and size
Of the toffees
That came in gold paper,

One would be pressed
Big and old
Into my sweaty paw.

They were a weight;
Some would still
Carry a king's head.

Now I count out
The small ones,
Most the same dull brown;

Only a few gleam
Bright new copper,
Pushed by my finger

Into my open palm.
At the end
My hands need washing.

Margate

The waves
Smack my legs
And my toes
Sink deep
Into liquid sand.

I look
At the sea
And feel again
The cold
Slap of betrayal.

Scratching

My Leg itches at night.

My fingers sprout nails
To probe beneath

Down to lower layers
Down and down,

Scraping away
Bombed-out-house-rubble

Scraping away
Decades of cuticled

Chitinous scabbed-up
Festering betrayals.

My fingers scrape away,
Digging for the baby.

Long Slow Betrayals, Inge Schlaile

Baghdad Dust Storm, Patrick Howse

Baghdad

Two floppy-eared lambs
Moved in next door
To chomp their way
Through overgrown garden.

They had shared
Womb and placenta
And stayed inseparable,
Always side by side.

When all the scrub
Was converted to protein
One was killed
for a family celebration.

For long days
And hot tortured nights
The survivor wailed;
Until they killed him too.

Dollars

I watch my fingers
Smoothing out the bills,
Folding and easing out the crinkles;

They make a noise
Only they make.
I start to count;

I notice the bloodstains.

Blackbirds in Acton Park

Interior paths
Wander through
Spring sunlight

To a sudden
Chilling shade
Of chattering
Alarm.

For Phil Goodwin

Der Grund

Wheeled wailing down white
Walled corridors with neon
Strip lights and antiseptic smells

The doctors knew he'd retain
No memory of his trauma,
That he needed no maternal clutter.

Mercilessly, they helped him
Their hearts inured:
Sound bounced off clinical surfaces

Without ever penetrating
Medical ears, or reaching
His distant mother.

Early, very early he learnt
He was alone, and felt
The anger of the ignored;

And all his life he fought
Furiously to transform this
Curse into some kind of blessing.

Responsibility

(To the Nomenklatura)

Don't believe it involves chauffeur driven cars;
Please try not to confuse it with cascading
Emails of patronising ill-written bollocks;
Don't suppose it means asking your PA

To pick up your dry-cleaning,
Or creating new layers of lackeydom,
Or paying yourself whatever you like;
Above all, don't think it involves meetings.

Picture, instead, pacing around a hot and
Dusty office while you wonder
If the people you've sent out on a story
Will come back unharmed – or at all;

Imagine directing a cameraman in the pools of
Blood and urine left by a suicide bomber
("Don't bother with any close-ups –
We'll never use the body parts");

Think of telling him later that there
Just weren't enough dead
To interest the teatime news;
And listening as he describes

A baby smeared over a pavement
And splashed on a wall;
Then looking him in the eye
And persuading him what we do matters.

For Stu, Moose and Tim

Lying Awake

I will tell you anything
You might want to know:
Just please let me sleep.

Resistance is worn down by
Hours blinking in the
Eye-accustomed dark,

Trying to count sheep, or cats,
Or visited lands,
Or airports flown from,

Or perhaps to, because they
Aren't always exactly…
But anything to stop

The insurgent anxiety
Infiltrating the
Revulsion of the

Stoicism we all show in
The blood-drained face of
Other men's nightmares.

Horses Near Fort William

I walked alone that day
In shadow
Cast by mountains.

Where a solitary tree
Stooped to greet
A lead-grey loch

They waited side by side
Immense in their dignity,
Glossy black flanks

Rippling with latent power,
Noble heads tossing.
I gave them

Only soft words
And a gentle hand,
Touching a quiet acceptance

Of long days
And short lives
Faced together.

Not Wilfred Owen

In a Parisian building
That might be a sports centre,
There's what purports to be
Brancusi's studio.

Someone has chosen
Which objects to show,
And neatly arranged them;
They look like they're dusted every morning.

Told to behave, everything
Seems to be here:
The shapes in plaster,
The inspiring driftwood discoveries;

But it's edited, selected,
And presented to us –
This is a committee's view
Of the atelier, not the real thing.

Once poets crouched in trenches,
Winced at shell-bursts, and
Watched men's faces
As they died in agony,

Devils sick of sin.
Now they watch television,
Electronically stimulating outrage,
their pity distilled vicariously,

Experience confused with viewing,
Visceral reality muddled with image.
They watch war on the news
And think that's enough.

Death

There's too much noise
For Darwinian comfort:
As the robins bring grubs

To the bushes beneath the window
They bring attention to themselves.

Half noticed but completely predictable
A cat pours himself into
The garden like treacle,

And black expectant Death
Waits quietly in the shadows.

Now with an immature flurry
A fledgling flaps onto the fence,
Scruffy down poking through

Brown plumage, his gaping gullet
Taking a parental stream of food.

It can't last long:
Overbalancing he falls
With a frantic chatter:

Instantly a thump of cat
On wooden planking stuns him

Into astonished passive acceptance
Of the clamped whiskered jaws
On his choking throat.

Returning, a bewildered parent
Chirps in vain for a hungry mouth.

Shadow Cast by Mountains, Inge Schlaile

PART II
A New Life

Red Never Seems to Dry Completely

(What the artist told me)

She paints like an otter swims:
Instinct, bold and lithe, guides her
Capture of elusive glinting expression.

Now in the heart of her canvas
An expansive splash of violence
Reveals to me an eternal truth

Even in baking Levantine sun,
Even on hot absorbent stone,
Red never seems to dry completely.

Patrick, PTSD, 2010, Inge Schlaile

Explaining Love to an Astronomer

An explosion
Fills an empty universe
With light and debris

Life begins

First Aid Lecture

To avoid
Constriction

Remove the
Wedding ring.

For Matt Webb

NBH

Playful stones thrown
By small children
Bounce harmlessly
Off our backs.

Now bullets skip
In the ruins
Of the freshly
Flattened homes;

And a tree stands
Alone among the
Concrete Rubble,
Growing green.

* * * * * *

I'm running by the river
That watered Eden;
Its reeds whisper
Of Babylon.

A body is dragged up the
Stone embankment;
It leaves a wet
Brown stain behind;

It stares to heaven, looking
In vain for mercy,
A round hole drilled
In its forehead.

* * * * * *

Hour after hour I find
New ways to say
The soldier's head
Was hacked off.

Sigmund Freud's Vienna Home

Thirty years after Freud
Was forced to flee for his life,
An Austrian Chancellor

Was pointedly asked
(in the United States)
Why Vienna had forgotten him.

Like his patients perhaps,
This museum was conceived
In acute embarrassment.

Only echoes of his presence are present
In his photographs and books,
And in some of his possessions

That were allowed to come back,
Even though he never could.
And up the hill from the Freudhaus

A one-way street is marked
With the usual no-entry sign;
There, too, posts are painted

With two red stripes
Separated by white.
I mistake them for the Austrian flag.

Evening in the Biergarten

The sun climbs the wall
Chased by shadow.

She was beautiful
Twenty years ago,

But you can only tell
By the way she looks at others:

She still expects
To be adored.

Dusk embraces her,
Night comes.

Gewitter

The Munich night
Blazes with lightning,
Striking again and again
Illuminating the full sky,

Searing light scorching
Through the rain,
Through the darkness,
Through bodies, almost
X-rays, showing bones.

The streets run
In monsoon torrents,
And still the clouds
Shine brilliant,

Bashing light,
Hammering electricity
Into the earth,
Pummelling sparks
Into holes left by hailstones.

Each blow must be the last,
Yet always another comes.
Breath is expelled
By the static in my lungs,

By the power surging
Through my heart
Through my veins
Through my blood

Into my soul.

For Inge

Monte Estoril

The old stone breakwater
Proudly juts from Portugal
Almost to Brazil.

Alone, our legs dangle lazily
Kicking to remind us
That they still work.

Between our toes, deep green
Reflections and shadows play
With reflections of shadows;

Purple spectres chase
Mermaids, twisting and
Writhing through translucence

As smoke snakes and curls
From fire through air,
Bleeding hypnotically away.

Glancing out further,
Infinite shades of silver-blue
Grey to the horizon, to ships.

But at our feet,
At the end of Europe,
Light is not allowed to escape:

It soaks in;
It dissolves.

Inge Schlaile

Anti-Natal Clinic

'Do you
know where you live?'
She's been talking to her
Colleagues, well gossiping really
And it makes no difference to her
That my partner has two masters degrees
And speaks seven languages
She's pregnant and here
So she must be a bit
stupid.

We've
Interrupted
Her talk to ask where
We should sit:
Over there.

We
stay over there
While they chat behind their
Wall-like desk and closed faces.
An hour and a half later
We're told what not
To eat

And
What not
To do
And

How
Not to travel
And just what can
Go wrong if you eat
Peanuts or shellfish or sushi
Or if you're too old
Or if there's
A history
Of

High
Blood pressure
And her teeth might fall
Out and she might have spotting
If she cycles or makes
Love at all
And

There's
The risk of Down's Syndrome
Which is not a
Diagnostic
But

A
Probability
And have we thought
What we'd do if it was negative
Which doesn't mean in
This instance really
Negative
But

Really
Positive
And when you
Look out of the window
You can just see Wormwood
Scrubs
And

Yes
I'm aware
You should spell
It with an
'e' .

Clara, 16th August 2012

I don't want this day,
Her first day,
To ever end.

She practices facial expressions,
Trying them out,
Not sure what they're for.

Her eyes open
And fight for focus,
Beginning the long

And perhaps futile
Attempt to make
Sense of the world.

Tomorrow she can be dressed
In her mortality,
And in mine;

Tomorrow she can start
The long process
Of imperfecting herself.

But this day,
Her first day,
Stands outside time.

An Autumn Baby

I only have her
For the morning.
Later she can
Enjoy to the full
Everything the day
Can bring her.

She has places to go,
People to see,
And others to love;
This is my hope.
It's her spring,
But my autumn.

So I wish for a
Golden day of leaves
Falling deeply into
A fruitful country;
Because I only have her
For the morning.

For Clara

February Thaw

The trees blossom
With snow.

The petals fall
In blizzards,

By the sun
Brought down;

On warm earth
They melt.

Winter hurls back
Hushed fury,

Flowering brilliant white,
Burying spring.

Salzburg

This fabric of woven cloud
Makes the surrounding
Mountains purely theoretical

And even the unbroken threads of rain
Unravel the blanket greyness
Too slowly to lift the gloom.

The high blue Alpine skies
Where the white summit waves break
Sit beyond the range

Of sight or foresight:
You could be forgiven
For thinking it will last forever.

Flint

Lumps of chalk lie jolted
from cliffs, tide-washed
and rounded by salt,

pitted till they crumble,
allowing adamant flint
to cut its way free;

I find a piece, stumpy
as a cut sapling log,
glass-backed planes

shining glossy wet
in autumn sunshine.
This is a rock

to build walls from,
to hide behind,
to repel all attacks.

Slowly, away from its sea,
the shattered-mirror
facets cloud and fade.

In a Spring Garden

Sulphurous flowers explode
From bare twigs
Unruffled by breeze

Yet manically twitching
With the frequent weight
Of sparrow or wren.

Where holly and ivy
Grow together in shade
Clamorous blackbirds display

On territorial borders,
Imprinted fear fed by
Eternally staved-off hunger.

The Waves

The waves diminish slowly,
a tide retreating from a brutal flood;
Where once I stood and felt their
shocking cold slap on my chest,
And feared my feet would be swept from under me,
Now they splash playfully at my toes,
their menace gone,

Snakes without fangs,
or yet to learn the art of venom.
Only faint echoes of the overwhelming,
unstoppable incoming rush
That swept on mercilessly,
taking everything away with it, and leaving
Me gasping, drenched and naked,
lashed by the double-edged luck of the survivor.

Passing My Old Home

It's winter
But I smell
Lilac blossom:

The scent of
A past spring
When I left her.

I shiver,
Expecting
To meet myself.

Clara and the Pencil

She grips a pencil
Better than a spoon.

Slowly lifted,
Then expertly held
In stubby fingers,

Loops and lines
Flow from hesitancy
To freedom,

Crafting the
Common ancestor
Of poetry and art.

It has meaning
I can't see.

Munich Christmas Market

The old lady waits cold,
Bundled in thick protecting layers
Against fat swirling snowflakes
Settling around mulled wine stalls.

She greets her daughter
With an embarrassed smile,
The shuffling of numb feet,
And an eyes-averted handshake.

Lying between them
A baby can be glimpsed
Through the clear plastic
Of a pram's raincover.

On the Overgrown Path

The autumn woodland sun
Slashes shadows through
Bramble strangled bracken;

Undergrowth long checked by
The slow repeated
Steps of generations

Now springs forth anew,
Nourished by cheap
And careless killers

Lying silent, patient for
The foot that
Fulfils their destiny.

Children of men unborn
When that war
Was long forgotten

Will play between trees
In a forest
Of legendary horrors,

Moving mossy red stones,
Ending their game
Abruptly.

For Stuart Hughes

Orkney Mainland

Northern sunlight entices
Gentle hills into seas
Where companionable seals swim,
Ripping fish apart.

Rings of stones speak
In tongues long forgotten
But still understood,
And neolithic certainties shelter

Beneath turf mounds so old
The earth grew up with them
To the late-coming laughter
Of Vikings.

Hen harriers follow me,
Pale ghosts unseen,
A lilt on the wind
And shadows in the grass.

A Fable

Burdened eternally with living
In a myth,
He pulls behind his thin
And bent body

A huge rounded boulder, attached
With a chain
To his vein-strained muscle
And taut sinew.

Up mountains as steep and
Mystical as Olympus
The load is dragged, step
By tortured step:

Bleeding toes slip and scrape into
Pitiless stone paths
Until the brief summit plateau
Brings fleeting relief.

Now, with the downward slope
The rock becomes
A projectile, stunning, flattening and
Pulling him down,

Weak, battered and at last unconscious,
A broken man.
He wakes at the bottom and blinks,
Astonished by sunshine.

Burford Leveller

Death was a great terror to him, as unto most

Low sun kisses Cotswold stone.

The gently rising river
Spills slowly over its bank
Watched by a little girl
Feeding ducks.

Outside the church,
Pitted by bullets,
A musket-scarred wall
Makes the Leveller's case.

Madrid: Lorca's Statue

I look at him
Trying to remember.

He holds a bird
In his hands

And children pause
Play to embrace him.

The defiant November
Sun shines warm

As a woman
Thrusts a red carnation

Under my nose
And harangues me

In a language
I don't understand.

Drawing in the Sand

With a stick
the little girls
scrapes lines,

patterns on
the jetty, five
times her length

in all directions.
A man asks
what it means;

perhaps we'll
know when it's
finished. Darkness

falls and she
works on in
determined strokes.

Helios

The smudged sun dips
To stain the city gold,
Anointing the little girl
With glory.

For the first time
She recognises the charioteer
God, and speeds him away
With a wave and a blown kiss.

She has the joyous instincts
She was born with;
Her cast shadow
Hides my face.

For Clara

Hug

Man and woman
And baby embrace.

For an instant,
It stops the world:

At the sound of
Slave traders' whips,

With the approach
Of invading armies

On the train
To Auschwitz,

Cavernous shadows
Are chased away

By lightning, and
Somewhere a new

Universe is born,
Founded on love.

Returning My Gas Mask

Rediscovered in a shed,
A relic of the excitement
Of going to war in the desert
Just like my dad.

Carried through unforgiving corridors
Narrowed by latte-fuelled careers,
Finally it is handed in
Nine years late.

All I get in return
Is my acceptance of a limit,
The walled-in admission of a hope
That I have done my war.

Isar

The water dashes
over my dangling feet
straight from the river,
straight from the mountains;

On the hottest day
of my short summer
I fear the coldness
of the clear stream.

Maria Einsiedel Bad

Straight from a river
Straight from mountains,
The water is
Too icy for me,

Baby and mother
Splash away,
Smiling and waving,
Receding.

Holding on,
Heading off,
Further, colder into
Remoteness,

Unstoppably into
Darker depths,
Forever further
Into distance.

Hoy from Orkney, Patrick Howse

Hoy Beach Stone

White and smooth,
Pocketed flat and small.
The Kittiwakes squat
In sandstone cliffs,

Decaying red tenements
Rented by lonely puffins.
Skuas patrol sea-sky
And the heather beyond,

Guarding the rare,
Endangered silence.
I kiss the stone
And throw it out to sea.

Metamorphosen

Browning horse chestnuts
Cast dappled shadows
On wooden tables.

Beautiful women cycle
To drink beer
From litre glasses;

Men in lederhosen
Embrace traditions older
Than their grandfathers;

Richard Strauss vainly
Yearns to restore
What they've lost.

Three Paris Pictures

I. Rue de la Folie-Mericourt

Sunlight warms wrought iron balconies
And an elegant stone facade;

Through a narrow gap
Between decaying curtains
A fleeting reflection of swifts
Proclaims spring in a splash of sky.

II. Inge in the Bathroom

Almost touchable, she stands naked
With swollen breasts and proud pregnancy;

The cheap hotel light
Etches new blue veins,
Radiating elemental beauty
Beneath thin translucent skin.

III. Metro to the Gare du Nord

An ugly old woman squeezes
'La Vie en Rose' from an accordion;

Braced against the jarring train
Her gorgeous smile recognises
My acknowledgement
That every parting is a little death.

The Scream

Gurgling in high-chair,
Bashing a plastic spoon,
She displays her two teeth
When she laughs.

She tries out sounds
To see what they can do,
Learning the ancient spell
That turns noise to language.

Then, perfectly pitched
To white light,
She experiments
With a scream.

Part of my innermost ear
Which, lying deep,
Wants only to die,
Is kicked brutally alive.

Now, it's hot, now
Dust mingles in the air
With the urine-petrol taste
Of bomb in my throat.

Bouncing round my skull,
Pain brings me back,
Blinking I return
To the baby chuckling,

Biting her spoon
And tugging at her bib,
Delighted with the power
Of her voice.

Mint Imperials (the Jutland Veteran)

The old man offers me
Round hard sweets
From a paper bag:
It crickles, they rattle
Against one another.

He chuckles at
The small boy me,
Extolling mints and pipes and hours
Spent scanning for patterns in
Oceanic depths of time,

Sitting, day after day
looking at the sea,
A knitted red blanket
Around his knees,
Remembering war.

Avalanches of spume
Tumble down the face
Of waves crashing ashore,
Headlong reckless advances,
Achieving only tactical success;

Further out the white
Crests appear randomly,
Suddenly punctuating
The grey green-grey-blue
As it smudges the skyline.

I start, finding myself offered
Round hard sweets
From a paper bag
By a little girl surfing
Oceanic depths of time.

Sunshine and Shadow, Madrid

Bright and warm
Rioja
Marisco y mixta
Streets crowded with noise,
Women who stare back,
My love's embrace;

Stars in a dark Sky.

Early morning
Stunned
Quiet clear, promising
Later heat; cracked
Cement-patched tiles;

Satellite dishes.

Crumbling cream
Render
On unrenewed buildings,
Bangs suddenly back
(Waiting for the next one);

Human hatred.

Horribly human
Hatred:
There is no escape
From bombs placed
Callously in markets.
There is no escape.

Terror

Alarms cry out loud
in shrill screams
of pain,
anguish,

and of excitement;
their echoes
drown out
reason.

But true fear
whispers.

Terror, Inge Schlaile

Oktoberfest Parade

I. Teams of horses tinkle
With burnished harness
Pulling drays of stacked barrels

And women in dirndl waving,
No longer at me,
But at younger men.

II. A woman's empty balcony
Commands a view she shuns,
Listening only to the bands

And the cheers through
half-open windows,
She smokes herself

Slowly to death,
Trapped in her room
By her childhood.

III. Children in carousels
Spin in delighted circles
Too small for me,

Loosening my desperate grip
On the corpse
Of what once was.

Treatment

Probing, scraping, scratching,
Each delicate twitch
A scything sweep.

Clattering mirror, drill,
Forceps bloody
On white enamel,

Life's lumped accumulation,
Debris, pain,
Deeply excavated.

The creaking tooth's
An old tree
In the felling gale.

I take it home with me.

The Crow with the Broken Wing

Black-smooth sleekness
Mocked by drooping
Feathered fan trailing
Through dust.

Seagulls are pecked
Viciously, a fox
Skirts by warily –
For now:

Hopping on through
Jarring pain, snapping
Up scattered morsels,
Defending doomed

Flawed-life-agony
With every skip,
Every gasping
Tortured breath.

Letting Go – Alpendohle

I stand on tortured twisted rocks
Two and a quarter miles above
The surface of the sea they were born in.

A cloud of ice crystals blasts my burning face.
I'm alone but for a happy flock of Alpine choughs;
Black as treacle, glossy as liquorice

They wheel and loop through the thin air,
Swirling round my head to make me dizzy,
Plunging from cliffs to make my heart skip.

But one of them stands with me
Yellow beak pointing defiantly into the Firn,
The wind that begs and bullies him to fly.

He fights the upward impulse stubbornly,
Perching on the edge of the world,
An arm's length away from me,

He walks to stay still, always blown backwards
Until finally he relents, and releases himself;
Just by stretching out his wings

He's pulled heavenwards instantly,
Riding every fluke, soaring in wildness,
Letting go, he embraces his thrilling element.

My Autumn in Munich

Morning stumbles bleary
From early mists
Into a sunshine
Stripped of warmth.

Dew soaked banks
Sparkle, and fractured
Shards dance between
Coots on a khaki pond.

In the Biergarten
Horse chestnut leaves
Lie in brown drifts
On wooden tables.

Tonbridge

The path shimmers in sunlight
Filtered by shivering branches.

Scudding clouds throw the fallen
Leaves into sudden darkness

And somewhere beneath the shadow,
A spider injects venom.

The Bankers' Mistake

They forgot
The money
Isn't theirs.

Satsuma

She's squeezed between
Lap and table
While I peel fruit.

Eating it myself
Would provoke
A violent reaction

Of yellow sludge
Expelled, as if
In protest

At the times
I ate breakfast
Listening

For the first
Bomb of the
Long hot day.

Innocent,
She eats segment
After segment.

The Baby and the Blue Plastic Bottle

She was first attracted by
Straight-from-the-fridge
Coldness against teething cheeks;

Later, she played with it
Empty cracking and crackling,
Biting and squeezing,

Fists and feet fiercely
Embracing the last night
Of her first trip to Italy.

Perhaps, as the last living
Witness to events skipping
Elusively before her memory,

That same colour blue
Suffused with sunlight shining
Might pierce her heart

With a joy, a sadness
As vibrant as the brush of lips
Or the scent of lavender,

And will move her profoundly
For one exquisite moment
She won't be able to explain.

Indian Summer

A white feather balancing
On a slender leaf.
The autumn wind blows.

The Abdication of Juan Carlos

In the harbour
An old clinker-built boat
Rose, and now falls
On the swell.

Once brightly painted
In green, perhaps,
Or dark blue,
It gamely braved

The Mediterranean seasons,
From the foulest wind
To the freedom
To say just how naked

An emperor might be.
But beneath the waterline,
Out of sight,
Timbers rotted.

(Barcelona, June 2014)

The Pursuit of Happiness

Garrulous choughs gather in the valley
As dawn etches rose and violet gullies
On frost-shattered peaks.

They begin a chaotic ascent
Climbing to cross the shadow-line
As it crawls down the mountains.

They indulge their aerobatic urges
On slopes just beyond me
Always enticingly out of reach.

Quicker than my weary earthbound limbs
Forever they are exactly
Somewhere that I am not.

I give up the chase and my gaze
Drifts into the meringue panorama
Of blue and white distance.

Then in sudden glossy-black nearness
The choughs play joyously round my smile
In the pure Alpine air.

While the Glacier Melts, Inge Schlaile

While the Glacier Melts

A splinter of crescent moon sets
Between chiselled peaks
As stark sun picks out torrents
Of liquid light.

They shuffle ahead, inner hands entwined,
Outer clutching sticks:
Birch and pine coldly shade their
Broad, level track,

She sings him old-child songs;
The Alpspitze soars
Across the valley, but his wits
Wander other paths.

The Couple in the Sauna

It's a German sauna
So no one here
Wears even a towel.

From the hairy old
To twenty-somethings
With their discrete tattoos

And pert round breasts
(Well, I'm only human),
And the strutting men

Whose self-confidence arises
As self-evidently as
The reason for it.

But it's the man
In the wheelchair,
And yes, the woman

Radiating a quiet grace
As she pushes it,
That I'm drawn to.

Naked, he looks rich:
Well-groomed, silver hair
His groin clean-shaven;

Her lovely auburn hair
Flows down to her
Firm and toned body.

Serenely she propels him
Before lowering the chair,
Bump after gentle bump,

Down the stone steps,
Then empties him out
Into the tepid pool.

He swims, paddling smoothly
With strong muscular arms;
She sits and waits

Tenderly accepting his head
Into her beautiful bosom,
All bitterness and shame

Sweated out on benches
In scalding hot rooms
With foot-burning marble floors,

And guilt blasted away
By jets of steam.
But their grief remains,

Floating on the water,
Hanging in the air,
What's left is love.

Vaughan Williams

I am welcomed into a community
Twenty generations deep.

A friend embraces me
And with infinite kindness
Whispers:

Life is sad.

Consolation is offered,
That doesn't cheer,
But does comfort:

Life is also beautiful.

The end is the silence
At the end.

Stranger

Was it
Just misery

Or was it
An illness

She cured
Sharing mountains?

A stranger smiled
And embraced me.

A Dream

There is sun after rain,
dazzling the washed-out
muted colours of memory.

A skinned-knee boy
stands patiently, socks
crumpled down to his

good, scuffed shoes;
looking right and left
and right again

the girl arrives hesitant,
but lets instilled worry
be brushed aside;

they hold hands and walk,
then run in the direction
of his assured nod,

over cobblestones shining
silver beneath brilliant
blue skies washed clean.

For Desmond and Margaret Howse

The Waiting Room

Shoulder to shoulder they sit
Packed into fixed seats
In two facing rows,
Unwilling to speak above a whisper.

Mostly, they're the victims
Of a cruel accident,
The unexpected and inadvertent
Arrival of their old age.

The one on the end
Wears old man's trousers,
And his pale socks bulge
With swollen ankles and feet.

He has waited here too long,
And abruptly tries to rise,
Creaking painful joints
To coax into flow stagnant blood.

He taps the floor between
Tentative shuffled steps,
Hoping life will return
Before his pending x-ray.

Apologetically, he smiles patiently
To the waiting room, murmuring
Through expiring breath
"It's only a matter of time".

Southport

The sea
Always seemed
A long way off.

It clings
To Lancashire
Like genteel poverty,

Terrified
By the ugly gaping
Maw of Liverpool:

Fleetwood was fish,
Blackpool vulgar,
Morecambe depressed;

But Southport
Was not Merseyside,
It was respectable.

I return
Always to one visit,
My son on my back,

My daughter
Holding my hand
Only when compelled to,

Crashing hard
Into a blue-rinse
Who looked down,

Then up
Into my soul
To foretell:

That one
Will one day
Break your heart.

For Eleanor

A Lion Lives With Me

Normally he sleeps,
Under my desk,
Or in the wardrobe,
Or under the kitchen table.

There are times when
I hear him snoring, purring,
Or flicking his tail,
Just to remind me he's there.

When he's awake,
He's very easily distracted
With music or films
Or a really good book.

There are times when
He behaves like a Tom Cat,
Pissing on the beds
And howling all night;

Then he keeps me awake,
Making me notice him,
Making me show him
The respect due to a lion.

And sometimes he becomes
A slavering Man-eater,
Who has to be faced-down
With a chair and whip.

He's quite a smelly
Old lion, and I often wish
That I could get rid of him;
But he's mine for life.

Relativity

Speeding emergency lights
Fleetingly reflected in
The polished pipes on a bar
Are the colour of a toy
My father bought me.

Listening to a rocket
Wail its way through
A dust storm
Took as long
As my childhood.

Amsterdam

Endless bikes jolt on
Rattling cobbles
Mirrored in sunlight
Shattering water,

And suddenly vinyl-popping
Breasts beckon
To trade that mostly
Passes by.

After the Tantrum

Four years'
unbrushed hair
sparked savagely

At the failure
to put tissues
back in a box;

The injustice
of impossibility
consumed her.

Now tear-moist
eyes, suddenly
as wise as

Aeschylus,
tell me gravely
to be kind.

For my daughter

Stained Glass (Brussels Cathedral)

Walls of brilliance
Cast eloquent light
Through the swords

Of knights hacking infidels;
A saint is cradled,
As if to comfort,

While axes and clubs
Steady in tight fists,
And a man in vivid blue

Slumps to the ground
Stricken, not by the dagger
In the closed hand

Of a bearded grim-faced
Murderer, but by the long blade
Of a thug in medieval green.

In such mysterious ways
The faithful conclude
God is love.

A Mass for Adi Schlaile

I need no permission,
I crave no praise.

Today, I do strange things:
I press my trousers;
I go to church;

There are candles,
Bells and incense,
Holy water, and the sign

Of the cross,
Made by my lover;
I kneel, while they pray

I say goodbye
In the silence a small
Child cries and

I write.
R.I.P. Adolf Schlaile, 1935-2016

Baselitz at the Haus Der Kunst

Eagles plummet
From dark skies
On walls built
To Imprison.

Hitler squats on
Heaps of ordure,
As blacks and
Greys and splashes

Of red fight
Mondrianic caricatures
Of swastikas, and
A little girl

Runs from room
To room, helping
Paint wash away
The stain.

Beyond my window

sea embraces sand
and waves wait their turn
to dissolve rock.

The universe expands
from every point at once,
its centre lies within us all:

nothing is forever,
but every second
Is packed with eternity.

Walking Towards Distant Mountains

They retreat forever
From futile steps
And hide behind
A sudden wood.

Spider-silk catches light
Beside untrodden paths
That wind through pines.
In touchable branches,

Resplendent in white tummy,
A black pine marten
With shining eyes
Tufts and twitches his ears.

Stealthily a storm
Rolls in from the hidden
Jagged skyline, and
Snow begins to fall.

Inge Schlaile

PART III
A Winter Comes

A Winter Comes

A darkness descends
(Not an absence of light –
A thing of itself,
A creature of night),

And while the rain falls,
Turning swiftly to snow,
One by one cosy fires
Are extinguished and go

Cold in a season
That despises the kind,
Celebrates ignorance,
Exhorts only blind

Hatred and violence,
Suspicion and rage,
Dragging us down to
A savage Dark Age.

In-Ger-Land

Patriots!
you
red-crossed
wrapped and tanked
up tossers
of coins at kids
escaped from
wars
you can't
imagine

scorning
desperate
powerlessness

singing songs
glorifying
slaughter
gripped

by delusions
of shared identity
you believe
you own:

England
is
a
German
word.

Jewish Museum, Munich

A girl asks
'Even the children?'

I kiss
my daughter.

No one sees,
She sleeps on.

It is for them.

For Maureen

A Ragged Flag

I look upwards
to blue streaming
with scudding clouds,
and my nation's flag.

It flaps wildly,
rattling the metal staff
shrilly, arrhythmically,
a gunfire cracking

edge thrashes
torn and frayed,
as though from battle:
a colour to die beneath with pride.

Not this one:
a sunset ritual
proved too much effort
for its patriotic owner.

For Tim Mercer, 12th July

Black & White: Kindertransport Memorial

He asks me quietly
where metal ends
and flesh begins.

Grey hour-glass grains
pour out of history,
flowing from the bronze

Through his lens and eye,
and a mind hard-wired
by bearing witness;

His monochrome bleeds,
defining softly the colours
of the past's compassion

And the blank tones
of our own fear-
fuelled indifference.

For Chris Booth

Leaving Broadstairs

From my doorstep
A subtle dawn's
First pink wash

Disengages
From dense deep
Lead blue waves;

At the hilltop
The livid sun
Thrusts water aside.

A summer's end
Lights her face
When she wakes.

Refugee

I glimpse a graphite sea
Smudging a sky
Laden with menace.

I have sought escape
From my darkest dawns,
Abandoning precious things,

To wash ashore
Seeking help the fearful
Would dare to deny.

Nothing is ours
By right, permanent:
Every line is provisional.

Thanet

England ends
in layers of azure
shimmering
into silver
beside the golden sand,
fusing light,
sea and sky.

Pensioners
sit before their beach huts,
an inward-
gazing semi-
circle reddening at
the shoulders,
post-card-fat

with burned backs
spurning the horizon,
forgotten
grandchildren
playing in the wild surf.
Their kettle
starts to boil.

Overnight Snow

Spring burned in that fire
Behind the evening trees

All day it bled the ice
Back into lake and stream

And softly dropped the branches' burden
Wetly to the ground.

But insinuated with the coming dark
Recoiled winter lashes out;

Cold waves of cloud overwhelm
The night's velvet blueness

And the morning is white.

Overnight Snow, Patrick Howse

Seaside in Winter

Terraces emerge
In exposed rocks,
Furrows cut parallel
Into chalk.

The turn, the flood;
Waves crash
On sea wall
Rebounding, retreating,

Colliding into
Haphazard patterns
Too complex
To understand.

The seagulls
Sit on rooftops,
Snipers waiting
For a clear shot.

Secret Garden

Hidden corners open
Through a swinging gate
For bobbing pigtails,
Running around berried shrubs

To carved wood gorillas,
Climbing frames and swings,
While figs and vines and nuts
Feed respectfully quiet birds.

But the small girls
Feel the need to fill
The peaceful void
With screams.

The History Thief

Stair climbing
Nosferatu shadow

Soak-staining
Bleeding black

Into the very
Memory of sunlight.

The Storm

Wolves beseige us,
night howls dripping
with slavered flesh.

In the light,
branches lie torn
from a tree,

beloved by birds
beloved by me;
I stuff dismembered

limbs into sacks,
and sweep up
the scattered leaves.

Badger

Shrapnel bursts
Of mistletoe
Explode in trees

Stripped bare
By a war:
Winter has come.

White flashes
Nuzzle and snuffle
Through dead leaves.

I whisper:
Go deeper,
Go darker.

The Tide in Viking Bay

Lines of men
Die of thirst
In a desert,

Their white foam
Fingernails clawing
at the smoothed sand.

My boots press dryness
Out from my toes
In a subterranean wave

While above high-water
A little girl
Draws with a pointed finger.

When I look down
My feet are again
Engulfed by cold surf.

Washing Ashore

Line upon line
Waves crash in
An inexhaustible

Succession smashing
Against the shore,
Creating new coastlines,

A violence of
Expressive destruction,
Generation

After generation
Sweeping away
Marks in the sand,

Repeating the patterns
In ever-novel
Sequences, crying out

To be heard
Over the deafening
Roar of the sea.

Weissbier

The grumpy waitress is lashed
By the twang of Americans
Above the Bavarian hum,
Until the end of her shift.

He drools and dozes
In front of a beer
Three quarters drunk,
Years outstripped by age.

She taps his ruined hand;
Dazed, he blinks alive,
Dribble dripping from slack mouth,
Redness defining weary eyes.

Digging in his pocket,
He mumbles to her:
It's not death
That beats you;

It's life.

Fortress

Their bedroom
was protected,

with steel bars
on the windows.

When men came,
armed with darkness,

there was no
escape that way.

For Camilla Carr

The Whole of Human History

A man makes a pot…

He's learned his craft;
it's a good pot.

He paints the pot
and people admire it;
it's a beautiful pot.

Men with weapons
barge in, and
kill the potter,

then they smash
the pot to pieces.

A man makes a pot…

Cassandra

Offer truth
Knowing

It won't be
Believed.

Carousel

Parents look beyond
Their children

In a sudden trance
Of recall.

After the Storm

Distant bands of leaden blue
yield to limpid turquoise,
as sun exposes lilac wetness
to a merciless beating
on the unforgiving sand.

White still flecks the surf
rolling against the retreating tide,
turbulent yet depleted,
run out, like luck.
It is the end of something.

Crucifixion

It requires faith
to believe in
a virgin birth,

in resurrection,
in borrowed stories
with flimsy sources.

But the betrayal,
the indifference
of the powerful,
that mocking
crowd enjoying
the spectacle,

the cruel taunts,
an extra little agony
of a thorned crown,

a man inured
to the suffering
of others happily

hammering nails
into hands, the
heartbroken mother;

In His death,
in the manner
of His death,
in that I can believe.

Churchyard, St Peter's-in-Thanet

Wild flowers jostle
With uncut grass
To hush the gentle sleep
Of England's comfortable dead:

Old stones mark
Old people's graves,
Faithful wives, beloved husbands
Lying Till We Meet Again.

The distinct cries of
Gulls drag me beyond
The hedgerows
To flat featureless fields

Enclosed by houses,
Power lines and pylons,
Towards a soft blue sky
Fading away into haze.

Fishing Like Ted Hughes

I feel the attraction
of immersion
in a landscape,

a sinking release
into a wild valley
of seductive beauty,

the thrill of the chase
beneath a dream of eyes,
the gasping writhing

wet landed prey,
deep dilating pupils
of sweet near death.

But the deceit
of the lure,
pretence of fly

or dangled worm,
a pale maggot impaled
on a pitiless hook,

dishonest animal screaming
shorn of nature's excuses,
and a vain hope

cruel conceit can fill
a soul's empty quarter;
there are only victims.

Ramsgate

Archaic walls tower
above reflective
luminescent

green-blue
dissolving beneath
smug hulls of delusion.

In shirts
and shorts
old men

turn their backs
as autumn squalls
blow out the light.

This is no harbour,
no safe haven;
it's a drawbridge.

Broadstairs

Dickens lived at the top
Of chalk cliffs
Dominating the beach.

Lumps of pitted white stone
Wash ashore and crumble
With the pressure

That can be applied just
With thumb and forefinger.
On the sand

Big feet aid small hands
Building castles to chase
The ebbing tide.

A Broadstairs Dawn

An enraged newborn sun
Flares at the meeting
Of crushed silk sky
And elephant skin sea.

Grey-blue pulses
Slap the shore,
Insisting on the transience
Of bedrock.

Dawn

Gold slowly seeps
Into the forest;

Sun blesses trees
Waiting for winter.

9th November 2016

Leaf Blowing

A harsh croaking
cackle of crows
chases a goshawk

into woods pillaged
by unforgiving
winter winds.

A man strapped
to a noise
herds ill-disciplined

drifts of leaves
from lawns,
retreating to catch

the runaways
teased backwards
by the gale.

He doggedly loads
a little cart
using a shiny

bladed shovel
and drives away,
blithely redistributing

Autumn's bounty
back along the
cleared track.

2nd December 2015

Bampton

All my boyhood summers
soaked into church walls
primed by a thousand winters.
Comfortable fields surround,

welcoming as woollen blankets
laid over the cold memory
of Saxon borders thrust aside
by disputed allegiances.

Engines and rotor blades
chop a sudden brutal loudness,
as the craft of modern war
round the spire;

hawks and jackdaws drown
in the blue-white sky
and my hand lingers
on walls built to protect,

on walls built to contain.
Particles of sand crumble
into my palm and fall
on soil deeper than England.

Leaving

Silver birches
drape the setting sun
with a curtain
of fragmented gold.

Waves of woodland
fade away to mist
as the darkness
gathers lost treasure.

Legacy

Flowers wrapped
In the purple
Of their shadow.

We want
A scent
To linger.

Looking at my Arm for the First Time

Down from a cross-
Scarred infancy,
Hairs are brambles
On scrubland,

Wrinkles dried-up
Watercourses on Mars
Or in a desert;
A delta of veins,

A freckle, down further
To pale fingernails
With thin crescents
Of yesterday's dirt,

Knuckles of folded ape-
Skin and the shade
Of a child's accident
Across three fingers.

Mayflower

Alone
In a lawn
Of white

Yellow
Pink-purple
Stars.

I don't know
The name
Of anything.

Margate - Somme Centenary

It splashed
Turner
as he bathed
in the light.

It rolls in slowly,
slowed,
inevitable,
vicious;

Wave upon wave
pushing
forwards,
wave upon wave.

We had a chance
to ride
this tide,
to make it

solid
as ice,
as fluid
as sunshine.

Now it rolls in
slowly,
slowed, inevitable,
viscous.

1st July 2016

On the Train from Paris

The tower sinks
Into an evening
Gold country.

A sudden square
Cemetery, walled
From fertile fields:

Men fought here –
That's who they were;
Now they are gone.

Watches retreat,
Travelling from
Summer to autumn.

Passports

My first was a black
Imposing, imperial
Anachronistic relic;

Then came bright red
Cricket ball leather,
Gilt lion and unicorn

Opening up limitless
Fairy-tale possibilities
For adventure, before

Airports and queues,
And the stamps
To get into wars,

Gold all worn off
By sweaty palms
And greasy ones;

Dull-cracked travel-
Stained and faded,
It's due to expire.

For Vivien Marsh

Reculver

A skylark soars
Above downs
That end abruptly
In a tumble of clay.

The sea shimmers
Grey-lilac silver,
and foams onto
shingle beaches.

The church towers
Stand still alone,
Heritage shorn of
Doctrine, abandoned

To the crumbling cliffs,
Complacent England
Astride yet older ruins
Surrendered to the tide.

Spitfire

A buzzard, belonging, circles
sun in blue heaven,
covering comfortable green
white with blossom.

Sudden merlin thunder,
loud enough to shatter time,
roars from harsh history
to gentle warm horizon.

My dazzled eyes see more
than beautiful tapered wings
and young men's sacrifice,
distinguishing dying embers

of childhoods burned in buildings,
or frozen by winters
endured in houses without windows,
and cold dark fears forever

dragged through long lives;
I recognise the survivors' loss.
I know what war means,
I think.

Yet still I feel the thrill,
seduced by a glorious marvel
once again tearing
Kent's spring sky.

Greenland Shark

Two hundred summer
thaws come and go
before his cold-slowed
heart stops pumping

blood through gills
fed by barely liquid water
beneath the ice.

Sleeping seals,
Reindeer, polar bears
messily pass its rows of teeth
to be laboriously digested

into toxic muscle
that smells of urine
and poisons dogs.

Each has a parasite
clamped to its eyes,
eating from outside in,

transforming the half-dark
that birthed them
to blackness,
bit by bit.

As strange
as an alien,
as familiar
as a shaved face,

the monster glides
slowly down
to lightless depths.

RFK & Aeschylus

He took a short-cut
Through a kitchen;
An eagle dropped
A tortoise on his head.

My shoulder hurts
A little bit,
All the time,

And when I
Grew a beard,
It was grey.

Precious things
I could no longer carry
Have fallen away:

Drop by drop,
In the night,
In my despair

Wisdom has come
By the awful
Grace of God,

Against my will
I have reached
A settlement.

The Ides of March

Cold, but not cold
enough
to ice the lake.

Frosted air
lifts steams
from the still water

into a sky
translucent
with new sunlight.

For Margaret Howse

A Tear for a Stranger

The sea and
the ancient landscape
in skirled chords

of lament,
of profound protest;

then a silence
summoning surf,

wind through the grass,
and a tear for a stranger.

For Peter Maxwell Davies

The Tramp

A weather-beaten tanned
White-haired stoop
Drags him down
Steep streets to the sea.

Random shouts at gulls,
At affronted shoppers,
At embarrassed children
And raucous white vans

Defy ridicule and indifference
With incoherent commentaries
On everything catching
Wild yellow-stained eyes.

Crow

Level with me,
His tree top
Mirrors my perch.

Crow-black polishes
Jet feathers, precision
Beak transformed

From brutal meat
Cleaver to forceps,
Re-placing each filament.

Through autumn denuded
Branches I watch;
Satisfied, he shrugs

And launches himself
Into a wind
Bringing snow.

Three Meals in London

I. Sloane Square

A breakfast
near Tiffany's;
it's business.

It's not a job
interview he says
before the interview;

I don't know
what the job is.
Neither does he.

II. South Kensington

Lunch with my son,
half a head taller
than me.

We chat and we
eat hummus.
I buy myself

books, then one
for him, just like
I used to do.

III. St Pancras

Tea with Betjeman.
I peer through the
crook of his arm,

but even if his bronze
cheek was softer than
his recorded voice,

I wouldn't see what
he sees; there's a
poet in the way.

The Wave

Who gets to say
Where it started
Or where it might end?

The vast oceanic surge
Churned and rolled
Oblivious and unstoppable

Crashing on and on,
A miasma of mud
And yellow vapour

Washing away the ages,
Drowning even the
Stinging hot metal

And the vile lusts
That fuelled it,
Washing away the ages.

Somewhere between
A champagne morning
And a filth-lathered night

It crashed ashore,
Headlong and wanton:
But no one marked

The final height of the tide,
Or counted the grains of sand
Sucked back into the depths.

The Wife of Bath

Scattered shadow lies
Strewn across the park;
Veils and headscarves

Cover every woman's head
And living illustrations
From Chaucer speak

Arabic and Somali
Into smartphones.
On the see-saw

A smiling son
Balances my blonde
Daughter perfectly.

Tree Stump

Grub-sculpted mound
Etched with tunnels
In crumbling pulp,

Slowly nourishing
The consumption
Of its children.

Westpark (Winter)

Crows bore holes
Into the snow
With their beaks
And their blackness

War Cemetery, Ypres

In my sensitive youth
I felt the stirring,
In the air
And beneath my feet,
Of the unquiet dead.

Slowly the survivors
Sank beneath the weight
Of the years,
Bleeding into a common
Stain, faded yet indelible:

Earth and sky brokered
Peace in these woods and fields.
Only the stones,
The very stones themselves
Still speak.

For James Rodgers

Wild Geese

From a wet green-bleak world
Prone to storms they fled,
Whipped more by foul winds
Than helped on by fair.

Across a hundred hostile lands
They searched for something,
Something taken from them,
A vagueness that gnawed

Through any sense of home.
One by one their progeny
Descend from a sky clouded
By estrangement from everywhere.

On applying for Irish citizenship

Tegernsee

Radiant mists draw
shadow curtains across
the undefined meeting
of mountains and sky.

Coots leave blazing
wakes as shards of sunlight
sparkle brilliant,
fleeting silver on the water.

Soft plumes of smoke
rise from cosy stoves
by the cold still lake's
far distant shore.

Hope

Night engulfs us.
Only flickers remain,
Nurtured by shaking
Hands with scorched
Palms and backs
Lashed by wind.

Each tiny glimmer
Gives neither
Illumination,
Nor much heat,
But each is kept
Stubbornly alive;

Perhaps this
Is the one,
That one day,
Will be wafted
And fed to blaze,
A new torch

To lead us
Through our tunnel
Of black horror
As we stumble,
Blinking, towards
Distant sunshine.

Train to Strasbourg

The frosty sunset
Burns a livid hole
In the crushed
Silk sky.

We travel backwards
Past fields and woods
Fought over
In pursuit of peace

By every generation
Before my own:
We just surrendered
Without a fight.

Inge Schlaile

The Hundred Acre Wood

The gorse bushes
burst with brimstone
in prickly denials
of the cold dark winter.

Tall pine trees
crowd on hilltops,
conspiratorial
copses whispering:

Somewhere a
kind sun still shines
on endless summers
of small adventures.

Patrick Howse grew up in Lancashire and worked as a journalist for 25 years.

He covered conflicts in Northern Ireland and the Middle East, and between 2004 and 2009 was bureau chief for the BBC in Baghdad.

He now works as a writer, and trains conflict journalists from major international news organisations.

He divides his time between Britain and Germany, where he has found joy, inspiration and sanctuary among the landscapes and people of Bavaria.

Patrick holds dual UK and Irish citizenship.

Inge Schlaile was born in Munich, and studied Japanese at the city's Ludwig Maximillian University, before completing a masters degree in Organisational Psychology at London's Tavistock Centre,

She paints under the name Schlinge and has exhibited her work in California, London, Germany and Japan.